The Quotable
GEORGE WASHINGTON
*The Wisdom of an
American Patriot*

Compiled and Edited by
STEPHEN E. LUCAS

MADISON HOUSE
Madison, Wisconsin

Lucas, Stephen E.
The Quotable George Washington
The Wisdom of an American Patriot

LIBRARY OF CONGRESS CATALOGING-IN-PUBLICATION DATA

Washington, George, 1732–1799.
The quotable George Washington :
the wisdom of an American patriot /
compiled and edited by Stephen E. Lucas — 1st. ed.
p.   cm.
Includes index.
ISBN 0-945612-66-4 (alk. paper)
1. Washington, George, 1732–1799, Quotations.
2. Quotations, American.   I. Lucas, Stephen.   II. Title.
E312.79.W317   1999
973.4′1′092—dc21   99-27478

Printed in the United States of America
on acid-free recycled paper.

Published by
Madison House Publishers, Inc.
P.O. Box 3100, Madison, WI 53704
www.madisonhousebooks.com

FIRST EDITION

CONTENTS

To Patty

INTRODUCTION

WE DO NOT USUALLY THINK of George Washington as a man of words. Neither a gifted writer nor a captivating speaker, he lacked the stylistic felicity of Thomas Jefferson, the intellectual power of James Madison, the multifaceted genius of Benjamin Franklin, the rhetorical fire of Thomas Paine. Unlike the Lincoln and Jefferson memorials in the nation's capital, the Washington monument is inscribed with no words for the benefit of posterity. The two most famous statements attributed to Washington were never uttered by him. "I can't tell a lie" came from the pen of Parson Weems, who concocted the fable of the cherry tree in the 1806 edition of his fictionalized biography of Washington. The admonition against "entangling alliances" invoked for generations to forestall American involvement in world affairs was pronounced in Jefferson's first inaugural address.

Yet Washington was keenly aware of the power and importance of language. From the time of his entrance into the public arena at the age of twenty to his death forty-seven years later, he produced a steady stream of letters, reports, memoranda, addresses, messages, and speeches designed to express his views and to persuade people to them. As commander in chief of the American army during the Revolutionary War, he issued some

9,000 letters on military business, many of them of considerable length. He even proposed at one stage that the Continental Congress provide him with a portable press and a printer so he could keep up with "the multiplicity of writing and other business" that occupied so much of his time. Leading the army was as much a rhetorical as a military challenge.

At Mount Vernon after the war, Washington faced a staggering load of correspondence from America and abroad. It occupied so much of his attention that he often lamented the amount of time he was forced to divert from other matters to answer the letters he received. During the debates over ratification of the United States Constitution, he stayed in close communication with other Federalists, usually composing several letters a week to men of influence throughout the continent. As the first chief executive of the United States, he was responsible for a large volume of official correspondence, as well as for the usual range of presidential speeches and addresses. Nor did retirement provide much respite. Although no longer in public life, Washington was the most celebrated civic figure in the Western world. He continued to receive visitors at Mount Vernon and to maintain an active correspondence until his death in December 1799.

Just as Washington sought throughout his life to improve himself in other ways, so he worked to develop his skills as a writer. Although he never achieved—or aspired to—literary distinction, he did become a clear, forceful, economical stylist. A shrewd observer of people and events, he had a sharp eye for detail, and he was capable of producing richly textured narrative and descriptive prose. There are, for example, no more eloquent accounts in American literature of the suffering of the colonial troops at Valley Forge than in the letters written by Washington during the bleak winter of 1777–1778.

Washington also learned early in his career the importance of precision in discourse. As a young commander in the Virginia militia, he was deeply embarrassed by putting his signature to a public document that characterized as an "assassination" the death of a French emissary at the hands of Washington's troops in a frontier skirmish. Washington blamed his translator—an explanation that was better accepted in America than in Europe—but he never forgot the lesson that carelessness in language can have grave consequences.

One of the most notable features of Washington's discourse is his tendency to ground specific conclusions, decisions, and recommendations upon general principles. Like most people of the eighteenth century, Washington believed that human nature was uniform across the ages—that the motives, passions, fears, and ambitions which drove people to action in his time were the same as those that had operated for centuries and that would continue to operate for centuries to come. No matter what the subject, Washington's prose is studded with maxim-like statements that enunciate the principles governing his thought and conduct. Those principles reveal a great deal about the traits of character and judgment that made him, to borrow Jefferson's appraisal, "in every sense of the words a wise, a good and a great man."

In addition to telling us much about Washington himself, his writings have relevance beyond the eighteenth-century world in which he lived. His reading (which was more substantial than most historians have assumed), his life-long observation of people in everyday life, his decades of experience in politics and the military, his natural gifts and inclinations—all contributed to his astute grasp of human nature and powerful sense of practical wisdom. As we read his comments on subjects as diverse as government, foreign policy, and religious freedom on the one hand and friendship, character, and relations between the sexes on the other, we find that his words are often as applicable to our own time as they were to his.

We also find that Washington was considerably more human than is suggested by the stiff portraits, marble monuments, and moralistic biographies that have shaped his popular image. Although the bulk of his correspondence dealt with political and military affairs, a fair portion of it revolved around family business, personal relations, and the management of Mount Vernon. Notwithstanding the formal quality of his prose on virtually all topics—a trait that became increasingly conspicuous as he rose in public prominence and had to guard his words for fear of misinterpretation—we can see him in his letters struggling with many of the same everyday issues people have always faced. No matter how much he chided, for example, he could not save his wayward stepgrandson George Washington Parke Custis from neglecting his studies or squandering his financial resources. Yet his heartfelt directives to Custis—and to other family members—contain some of the most engaging prose in all of his correspondence. We can only lament that Martha Washington destroyed virtually all of his letters to her shortly before her death in 1802.

Of Washington's surviving letters, those to the Marquis de Lafayette are the most candid and the most relaxed in tone. The French aristocrat who came to America at the age of twenty to fight in the Revolution held a special place in Washington's heart. Childless, Washington came to regard Lafayette as a son; orphaned at the age of three, Lafayette came to revere Washington as a surrogate father. After Lafayette returned to France, the two men continued to correspond until Washington's death. Of the quotations in this book, twenty-nine come from letters to Lafayette—almost twice the number from letters to anyone else.

Other frequent correspondents include Washington's nephew Bushrod Washington; John Hancock, President of the Continental Congress during the first two years of the Revolutionary War; Joseph Reed, Washington's military secretary in 1775-1776 and subsequently a prominent member of the Continental Congress; James Madison, Washington's closest advisor at the outset of his first presidential administration; Alexander Hamilton, who succeeded Madison in Washington's confidence during the 1790s; Henry Knox and James McHenry, both of whom served in cabinet posts during Washington's presidency; and Henry Lee, a fellow Virginian and masterful orator who achieved a measure of literary immortality by eulogizing Washington as "first in war, first in peace, and first in the hearts of his countrymen."

Although the bulk of Washington's writing took the form of private correspondence, his most consequential words were those he expressed publicly. His speech to the potentially mutinous officers at Newburgh, New York, in the waning days of the Revolutionary War prevented that contest, in Jefferson's words, "from being closed, as most others have been, by a subversion of that liberty it was intended to establish." His circular letter to the governors of the thirteen states at the end of the war was widely celebrated throughout America, as was his speech to the Continental Congress resigning his commission as commander in chief. Six years later, his first inaugural address played a pivotal role in getting the government created by the federal Constitution off to a smooth start, while his annual messages to Congress throughout his presidency established a rhetorical tradition that, like the inaugural address, is followed to this day.

Washington's greatest public paper, his Farewell Address, ranks with the Declaration of Independence and the Gettysburg Address as the most honored of American political discourses. A valedictory in which

Washington set forth the tenets that should guide Americans in their relations with each other and with the rest of the world, it continued to be read in Congress each February 22 until the 1970s, and it has seldom been surpassed as a statement of the principles underlying the conduct of foreign policy. For generations it has been the most quoted of all Washington's public writings, a distinction it retains in this volume.

One of the perennial questions with respect to Washington is the extent to which his speeches and addresses were composed by aides and associates. This has been an issue ever since the early nineteenth century, when the public learned that Alexander Hamilton had been the principal draftsman of the Farewell Address. Burdened with a monumental load of official duties throughout his military and political careers, Washington often relied on the pens of other men. In this respect he was different from subsequent commanders and presidents only in the caliber of talent available to him. What other American leader has been able to include the likes of Hamilton and Madison among his speech writers?

Yet even on those occasions when Washington's addresses were crafted with the assistance of ghostwriters, the words, the ideas, even the syntax and diction, are unmistakably consonant with his own. Washington was far too concerned about his public persona and the potential impact of his discourse to allow anyone to compose for him without close supervision and correction. As president, for example, his typical method of speech preparation was to begin by soliciting recommendations from his cabinet about what topics should be discussed. Sometimes he would give these recommendations directly to the person responsible for drafting the speech. Or, working from the recommendations, he would draw up a list of main points with notes as to how they might be treated.

Once a draft of the address was prepared, Washington would review it, making changes in both the content and the manner of expression. At some stage, he would circulate the draft among his cabinet. If further changes were necessary, the process would continue until Washington had a text with which he was fully satisfied. Usually he would write out his speaking copy in his own hand, all the while smoothing, refining, and amending. It was a careful and time-consuming process in which Washington was actively involved at every stage and was ultimately responsible for the letter and spirit of the final text.

Perhaps the most intriguing of Washington's writings is the "Rules of Civility and Decent Behavior in Company and Conversation," which he transcribed as a school exercise sometime before his sixteenth birthday. The maxims expressed in these rules have been traced to a treatise composed by French Jesuits in 1595. Subsequently expanded and published on the Continent in at least five languages, they were printed in English about 1640 and went through eleven editions by 1672. The 110 rules copied by Washington were based on the English translation, but at some point they were simplified and reordered for use as a school exercise—by whom, we do not know. We do know, however, that the Rules of Civility influenced Washington long past his youth. Running a gamut of topics from courtesy, table manners, and correct speech to the importance of respecting other people and keeping alive "that little spark of celestial fire called conscience," they provided a set of principles that helped shape his character and conduct through the rest of his life. No collection of his sentiments would be complete without them.

BECAUSE OF WASHINGTON's towering status in American history, he has been quoted over the years in behalf of countless causes. Unfortunately, more than a few of the pronouncements attributed to him are either misstated or are outright fabrications. One of my aims in this book is to provide an accurate, reliable compilation that can be turned to with confidence. Every selection has been checked against one of three sources. Whenever possible, I have relied upon the University Press of Virginia's definitive edition of *The Papers of George Washington*, which to date has published about half of its projected eighty-five volumes of correspondence and addresses. For documents not yet available in this edition, I consulted John C. Fitzpatrick's thirty-nine-volume *Writings of George Washington* (1931–1944). I also relied on *George Washington's Rules of Civility and Decent Behavior* (1926), edited by Charles Moore. Long the standard scholarly work on its subject, Moore's book explicates the origins of the rules and presents a facsimile of them in Washington's own hand. (A new edition, prepared by Richard Brookhiser was published after I completed my research.) Whenever I had a question about the printed version of a document, I turned to the photostat of the original in the Washington papers at the University of Virginia.

While I have taken great pains to quote Washington's words accurately, I do not believe general readers should have to fight their way through the arcane conventions and sometimes baffling idiosyncrasies of eighteenth-century prose to discover his meaning. As with most writers, Washington would occasionally abbreviate words or omit characters—especially when composing in haste. Whenever he did so and his meaning is clear, I have silently added the missing material. In the interest of readability, I have modernized capitalization, spelling and punctuation, and I have eliminated Washington's underscoring when the emphasis is not integral to the meaning of his statement. Finally, I have identified the document from which each quotation is taken, the date of the document, and, if known, the location at which it was composed.

I have been fortunate to receive the aid and counsel of numerous people. John Kaminski, whose *Citizen Jefferson: The Wit and Wisdom of an American Sage* provided the model for this book, encouraged me to take on the project and read the entire manuscript with care and perceptiveness. So, too, did Greg Britton, the former director at Madison House, and Susan Zaeske, my colleague at the University of Wisconsin. Their advice regarding the content, length, and headings of individual quotations was invaluable. Richard Leffler read the introduction and offered a number of useful suggestions. I also benefited from the generous assistance of the staff at the Papers of George Washington, housed in Alderman Library at the University of Virginia. Dorothy Twohig, Philander Chase, and Frank Grizzard extended many kindnesses during my stay at Charlottesville, helped me track down a number of stray references, read portions of the manuscript, and responded to my queries with the depth of knowledge and insight that comes from dealing with Washington and his writings on a daily basis for many years. Mark Mastromarino also gave the introduction a careful reading.

Working from my manuscript, two research assistants, Teri Fair and Natalie Slater, located each entry in the published editions of Washington's writings, made copies of the relevant documents, and highlighted the appropriate passages so I could double check them for accuracy. Mary Dodge was responsible for entering the quotations on disk. This became an increasingly complicated task as more and more entries were added, as existing entries were lengthened, shortened or relocated, and as final corrections were made after each entry was rechecked for accuracy. Mary's work at each stage of this process was indispensable.

As always, I owe a substantial debt to my family—Patty, Ryan, and Jeff. They were especially helpful during the many stages of the decision-making process about the selections that should be included in the book and those that should be left out. Time and again they responded patiently to my requests for advice. The book is better as a result of their judgment and support—just as my life is better as a result of their love and fellowship.

Stephen E. Lucas
Madison, Wisconsin

George Washington Chronology 1732–1799

1732
Born at Pope's Creek, Virginia
(February 22)

1749
Appointed surveyor of
Culpeper County, Virginia

1753–1758
Officer in the Virginia militia

1758
Elected to Virginia House of Burgesses

1759
Marries Martha Dandridge Custis

1774
Delegate to First Continental Congress

1775
Delegate to Second Continental Congress

1775
Appointed Commander in Chief
of the Continental Army

1781

Accepts surrender of Lord Cornwallis
at Yorktown

1783

Presents Newburgh Address

1783

Issues final Circular Letter to Governors
of the Thirteen States

1783

Resigns as Commander in Chief
of the Continental Army

1783–1789

Private citizen at Mount Vernon

1787

Delegate to Constitutional Convention

1789–1797

President of the United States

1796

Issues Farewell Address

1797

Retires to Mount Vernon

1798

Accepts command of the American army
in event of war with France

1799

Dies at Mount Vernon
(December 14)

The Quotable

GEORGE WASHINGTON

Acquaintances

It is easy to make acquaintances, but very difficult to shake them off, however irksome and unprofitable they are found, after we have once committed ourselves to them.

To Bushrod Washington, Newburgh, January 15, 1783

Address

In writing or speaking, give to every person his due title according to his degree and the custom of the place.

Rules of Civility, 1745

Advice

Give not advice [without] being asked, and when desired do it briefly.

Rules of Civility, 1745

The opinion and advice of my friends I receive at all times as a proof of their friendship and am thankful when they are offered.

To Robert R. Livingston, Ramapaugh, June 29, 1780

I am anxious always to compare the opinions of those in whom I confide with one another; and those again (without being bound by them) with my own, that I may extract all the good I can.

To Alexander Hamilton, Mount Vernon, June 26, 1796

Agriculture

Agriculture has ever been amongst the most favorite amusements of my life.

To Arthur Young, Mount Vernon, August 6, 1786

I know of no pursuit in which more real and important service can be rendered to any country than by improving its agriculture.

To John Sinclair, Philadelphia, July 20, 1794

Ambition

There is no saying to what length an enterprising man may push his good fortune.

To the New York Council of Safety,
Philadelphia, August 4, 1777

How pitiful, in the eye of reason and religion, is that false ambition which desolates the world with fire and sword for the purposes of conquest and fame.

To John Lathrop, Mount Vernon, June 22, 1788

America

... an asylum for the poor and oppressed of all nations and religions.

General Orders, Newburgh, April 18, 1783

However unimportant America may be considered at present, ... there will assuredly come a day when this country will have some weight in the scale of empires.

To Marquis de Lafayette, Mount Vernon, August 15, 1786

I had always hoped that this land might become a safe and agreeable asylum to the virtuous and persecuted part of mankind, to whatever nation they might belong.

To Francis Adrian Van der Kemp,
Mount Vernon, May 28, 1788

I hope, some day or another, we shall become a storehouse and granary for the world.

To Marquis de Lafayette, Mount Vernon, June 19, 1788

That the government, though not absolutely perfect, is one of the best in the world, I have little doubt.

To Catherine Macaulay Graham, New York, January 9, 1790

American Revolution

Our cause is noble; it is the cause of mankind!

To James Warren, Middlebrook, March 31, 1779

It will not be believed that such a force as Great Britain has employed for eight years in this country could be baffled in their plan of subjugating it by numbers infinitely less, composed of men oftentimes half starved, always in rags, without pay, and experiencing, at times, every species of distress which human nature is capable of undergoing.

To Nathanael Greene, Newburgh, February 6, 1783

The foundation of our empire was not laid in the gloomy age of ignorance and superstition, but at an epocha when the rights of mankind were better understood and more clearly defined than at any former period.

Circular to the States, Newburgh, June 8, 1783

At this auspicious period, the United States came into existence as a nation, and if their citizens should not be completely free and happy, the fault will be entirely their own.

Circular to the States, Newburgh, June 8, 1783

Nor would I rob the fairer sex of their share in the glory of a revolution so honorable to human nature, for, indeed, I think you ladies are in the number of the best patriots America can boast.

To Annis Boudinot Stockton,
Mount Vernon, August 31, 1788

The American Revolution, or the peculiar light of the age, seems to have opened the eyes of almost every nation in Europe, and a spirit of equal liberty appears fast to be gaining ground everywhere.

To Hector St. John de Crevecoeur,
Mount Vernon, April 10, 1789

Our revolution was so distinguished for moderation, virtue, and humanity as to merit the eulogium ... of being unsullied with a crime.

To John Hawkins Stone, Philadelphia, December 23, 1796

Americans

We are apt to run from one extreme into another.

To John Jay, Mount Vernon, August 15, 1786

Nothing but harmony, honesty, industry, and frugality are necessary to make us a great and happy people.

To Marquis de Lafayette, Mount Vernon, January 29, 1789

I am sure the mass of citizens in these United States mean well, and I firmly believe they will always act well, whenever they can obtain a right understanding of matters.

To John Jay, Philadelphia, May 8, 1796

Anarchy

There is a natural and necessary progression from the extreme of anarchy to the extreme of tyranny.

Circular to the States, Newburgh, June 8, 1783

Appropriateness

It is absurd to act the same with a clown and a prince.

Rules of Civility, 1745

Argument

Strive not with your superiors in argument, but always submit your judgment to others with modesty.

Rules of Civility, 1745

Contradict not at every turn what others have to say.

Rules of Civility, 1745

Army

The distinction between a well-regulated army and a mob is the good order and discipline of the first and the licentious and disorderly behavior of the latter.

To Israel Putnam, New York, August 25, 1776

The army . . . is a dangerous instrument to play with.

To Alexander Hamilton, Newburgh, April 4, 1783

The Arts

The arts and sciences essential to the prosperity of the state and to the ornament and happiness of human life have a primary claim to the encouragement of every lover of his country and mankind.

To Joseph Willard, New Windsor, March 22, 1781

To promote literature in this rising empire, and to encourage the arts, have ever been amongst the warmest wishes of my heart.

To the Trustees of Washington Academy,
Mount Vernon, June 17, 1798

Bad Company

'Tis better to be alone than in bad company.

Rules of Civility, 1745

Bad Habits

It requires time to conquer bad habits, and hardly anything short of necessity is able to accomplish it.

To Arthur Young, Philadelphia, December 5, 1791

Bargains

It is not the lowest priced goods that are always the cheapest—the quality is, or ought to be, as much an object with the purchaser as the price.

To Philip Marsteller, Mount Vernon, December 15, 1786

Battle

I fortunately escaped without a wound, though the right wing where I stood was exposed to and received all the enemy's fire. . . . I heard bullets whistle, and believe me there was something charming in the sound.

To John Augustine Washington,
Great Meadows, May 31, 1754

By the miraculous care of Providence that protected me beyond all human expectation, I had four bullets through my coat and two horses shot under, and yet escaped unhurt.

To John Augustine Washington,
Fort Cumberland, July 18, 1755

Beliefs

Men's minds are as variant as their faces.

To Benjamin Harrison, Mount Vernon, March 9, 1789

The views of men can only be known, or guessed at, by their words or actions.

To Patrick Henry, Mount Vernon, January 15, 1799

Blame

When a man does all he can, though it succeeds not well, blame not him that did it.

Rules of Civility, 1745

Which is most blameworthy, those who see and will steadily pursue their interest, or those who cannot see, or seeing will not act wisely?

To David Stuart, New York, March 28, 1790

It is not easy for a man to throw the first stone for fear of having it returned to him.

To William Pearce, Philadelphia, December 18, 1793

Boasting

With me, it has always been a maxim rather to let my designs appear from my works than by my expressions. To talk long beforehand of things to be done is unpleasant.

To James Anderson, Mount Vernon, December 21, 1797

Books

A knowledge of books is the basis upon which other knowledge is to be built.

To Jonathan Boucher, Mount Vernon, July 9, 1771

Borrowing Money

There is no practice more dangerous than that of borrowing money.

To Samuel Washington, Mount Vernon, July 12, 1797

Brevity

Let your discourse with men of business be short and comprehensive.

Rules of Civility, 1745

Business

System to all things is the soul of business. To deliberate maturely and execute promptly is the way to conduct it to advantage.

To James Anderson, Mount Vernon, December 21, 1797

Candor

Candor is not a more conspicuous trait in the character of governments than it is of individuals.

To Timothy Pickering, Mount Vernon, August 29, 1797

Capital Punishment

I always hear of capital executions with concern, and regret that there should occur so many instances in which they are necessary.

To James Clinton, Philadelphia, December 31, 1778

Caution

All except desperate men look before they leap.

To James Madison, Mount Vernon, June 8, 1788

Censure

Why should I expect to be exempt from censure, the unfailing lot of an elevated station?

To Henry Laurens, Valley Forge, January 31, 1778

Chaos

The greater the chaos, the greater will be your merit in bringing forth order.

To Philip Schuyler, New Windsor, February 20, 1781

Character

Good moral character is the first essential in a man.

To George Steptoe Washington, Philadelphia, December 5, 1790

It is to be lamented . . . that great characters are seldom without a blot.

To Marquis de Lafayette, Mount Vernon, May 10, 1786

Charity

Let your heart feel for the afflictions and distresses of everyone, and let your hand give in proportion to your purse, remembering . . . that it is not everyone who asketh that deserveth charity.

To Bushrod Washington, Newburgh, January 15, 1783

Never let an indigent person ask without receiving something, if you have the means.

To George Washington Parke Custis,
Philadelphia, November 15, 1796

Checks and Balances

No man is a warmer advocate for proper restraints and wholesome checks in every department of government than I am; but I have never yet been able to discover the propriety of placing it absolutely out of the power of men to render essential services because a possibility remains of their doing ill.

To Bushrod Washington, Mount Vernon, November 10, 1787

Cities

The tumultuous populace of large cities are ever to be dreaded. Their indiscriminate violence prostrates for the time all public authority, and its consequences are sometimes extensive and terrible.

To Marquis de Lafayette, Philadelphia, July 28, 1791

Clothes

In your apparel be modest and endeavor to accommodate nature, rather than to procure admiration.

Rules of Civility, 1745

Do not conceive that fine clothes make fine men, any more than fine feathers make fine birds.

To Bushrod Washington, Newburgh, January 15, 1783

Commerce

Commerce and industry are the best mines of a nation.

To Joseph Reed, Morristown, May 28, 1780

A people ... who are possessed of the spirit of commerce, who see and who will pursue their advantages, may achieve almost anything.

To Benjamin Harrison, Mount Vernon, October 10, 1784

The period is not very remote when the benefits of a liberal and free commerce will, pretty generally, succeed to the devastations and horrors of war.

To Marquis de Lafayette, Mount Vernon, August 15, 1786

Committees

My observation on every employment in life is that wherever and whenever one person is found adequate to the discharge of a duty by close application thereto, it is worse executed by two persons, and scarcely done at all if three or more are employed therein.

To Henry Knox, Mount Vernon, September 24, 1792

Complaints

Complaints illy become those who are found to be the first aggressors.

To James Madison, Mount Vernon, March 31, 1787

Congress

For heaven's sake, who are Congress? Are they not the creatures of the people, amenable to them for their conduct and dependent from day to day on their breath?

To William Gordon, Newburgh, July 8, 1783

Conjecture

Conjectures are often substituted for facts.

To George Washington Parke Custis,
Mount Vernon, June 13, 1798

Conscience

Labor to keep alive in your breast that little spark of celestial fire called conscience.

Rules of Civility, 1745

Conscience . . . seldom comes to a man's aid while he is in the zenith of health and reveling in pomp and luxury upon ill-gotten spoils; it is generally the *last* act of his life and comes too late to be of much service to others here, or to himself hereafter.

To John Price Posey, Newburgh, August 7, 1782

Contracts

The only way to make men honest is to prevent their being otherwise, by tying them firmly to the accomplishment of their contracts.

To Lund Washington, Middlebrook, December 17, 1778

Conversation

Let your conversation be without malice or envy, for 'tis a sign of a tractable and commendable nature.

Rules of Civility, 1745

Correspondence

To correspond with those I love is among my highest gratifications.

To Henry Knox, Mount Vernon, January 5, 1785

Letters of friendship require no study, the communications are easy, and allowances are expected and made.

To Henry Knox, Mount Vernon, January 5, 1785

I am become so unprofitable a correspondent, and so remiss in my correspondencies, that nothing but the kindness of my friends in overlooking these deficiencies could induce them to favor me with a continuance of their letters.

To Gouverneur Morris, Philadelphia, December 22, 1795

Courtesy

Be courteous to all, but intimate with few, and let those few be well tried before you give them your confidence.

To Bushrod Washington, Newburgh, January 15, 1783

Cowardice

A crime of all others the most infamous in a soldier, the most injurious to an army, and the last to be forgiven.

General Orders, Cambridge, July 7, 1775

Creating Government

To form a new government requires infinite care and unbounded attention; for if the foundation is badly laid, the superstructure must be bad.

To John Augustine Washington, Philadelphia, May 31, 1776

I think every nation has a right to establish that form of government under which it conceives it shall live most happy, provided it infracts no right or is not dangerous to others.

To Marquis de Lafayette, Mount Vernon, December 25, 1798

Custom

The people at large are governed much by custom.

To Henry Laurens, Gulph Mills, December 15, 1777

Danger

Men who are familiarized to danger meet it without shrinking, whereas those who have never seen service often apprehend danger where no danger is.

To John Hancock, Cambridge, February 9, 1776

It is unfortunate when men cannot, or will not, see danger at a distance; or seeing it, are restrained in the means which are necessary to avert . . . it.

To John Trumbull, Mount Vernon, June 25, 1799

Death

. . . that abyss from whence no traveler is permitted to return.

To Marquis de Lafayette, Newburgh, April 5, 1783

I thank you for your kind condolence on the death of my nephew. It is a loss I sincerely regret, but as it is the will of Heaven, whose decrees are always just and wise, I submit to it without a murmur.

To Bryan Fairfax, Philadelphia, March 6, 1793

The death of near relations always produces awful and affecting emotions, under whatsoever circumstances it may happen.

> To Burgess Ball, Mount Vernon, September 22, 1799

I will move gently down the stream of life until I sleep with my fathers.

> To Marquis de Lafayette, Mount Vernon, February 1, 1782

When the summons comes, I shall endeavor to obey it with a good grace.

> To Burgess Ball, Mount Vernon, September 22, 1799

Debt

To contract new debts is not the way to pay old ones.

> To James Welch, Mount Vernon, April 7, 1799

Deception

I hate deception, even where the imagination only is concerned.

> To John Cochran, West Point, August 16, 1779

We ought not to deceive ourselves.

> To Joseph Reed, Morristown, May 28, 1780

Defamation

To speak evil of anyone, unless there is unequivocal proofs of their deserving it, is an injury for which there is no adequate reparation.

To George Washington Parke Custis,
Philadelphia, November 28, 1796

Deference

In company of those of higher quality than yourself, speak not till you are asked a question.

Rules of Civility, 1745

Democracy

Democratical states must always feel before they can see: it is this that makes their governments slow, but the people will be right at last.

To Marquis de Lafayette, Mount Vernon, July 25, 1785

Despair

We should never despair; our situation before has been unpromising and has changed for the better; so, I trust, it will again.

To Philip Schuyler, Smith's Clove, July 15, 1777

Destiny

There is a destiny which has the sovereign control of our actions, not to be resisted by the strongest efforts of human nature.

To Sarah Cary (Sally) Fairfax,
Fort Cumberland, September 12, 1758

Difficulties

We ought not to convert trifling difficulties into insuperable obstacles.

To Marquis de Malmedy, Morristown, May 16, 1777

Dining

Be not angry at table whatever happens, and if you have reason to be so, show it not.

Rules of Civility, 1745

Disappointment

It is the nature of man to be displeased with everything that disappoints a favorite hope or flattering project.

To Marquis de Lafayette, White Plains, September 1, 1778

Discipline

Discipline is the soul of an army. It makes small numbers formidable, procures success to the weak, and esteem to all.

General Instructions to the Captains of Companies,
Fort Loudon, July 29, 1757

The best general advice I can give . . . is to be strict in your discipline; that is, to require nothing unreasonable of your officers and men, but see that whatever is required be punctually complied with.

To William Woodford, Cambridge, November 10, 1775

Discipline, more than numbers, gives one army the superiority over another.

General Orders, Morristown, July 6, 1777

The firmness requisite for the real business of fighting is only to be attained by a constant course of discipline and service.

To Samuel Huntington, New Bridge, September 15, 1780

Discontent

It is much easier to avoid disagreements than to remove discontents.

To John Sullivan, New Windsor, May 11, 1781

There are combustibles in every state which a spark might set fire to.

To Henry Knox, Mount Vernon, December 26, 1786

Against the malignancy of the discontented, the turbulent and the vicious, no abilities, no exertions, nor the most unshaken integrity are any safeguard.

To John Jay, Philadelphia, November 1, 1794

Dispatch

Good measures should always be executed as soon as they are conceived and circumstances will permit.

To Timothy Pickering, Mount Vernon, August 1, 1796

Disputes

In disputes, be not so desirous to overcome as not to give liberty to each one to deliver his opinion.

Rules of Civility, 1745

Liberality and charity . . . ought to govern in all disputes.

To Benjamin Harrison, Mount Vernon, March 9, 1789

Dissension

I am under more apprehensions on account of our own dissensions than of the efforts of the enemy.

To Benedict Arnold, Middlebrook, December 13, 1778

Divine Providence

See the wondrous works of Providence! The uncertainty of human things!

To Robert Jackson, Mount Vernon, August 2, 1755

The determinations of Providence are always wise, often inscrutable, and though its decrees appear to bear hard upon us at times, is nevertheless meant for gracious purposes.

To Bryan Fairfax, Valley Forge, March 1, 1778

[It] is not for man to scan the wisdom of Providence. The best he can do is to submit to its decrees.

To Henry Knox, Philadelphia, March 2, 1797

We know little of ourselves, and still less of the ways of Providence.

To Bryan Fairfax, Mount Vernon, January 20, 1799

Dreams

Tell not your dreams but to your intimate friend.

Rules of Civility, 1745

Drunkenness

By degrees it renders a person feeble and not only unable to serve others but to help himself.

To John Christian Ehler, Philadelphia, December 23, 1793

Drunkenness is no excuse for rudeness.

To George Muse, Mount Vernon, January 29, 1774

Duty

Three things prompt men to a regular discharge of their duty in time of action—natural bravery, hope of reward, and fear of punishment.

To John Hancock, Cambridge, February 9, 1776

There is one reward that nothing can deprive me of, and that is the consciousness of having done my duty with the strictest rectitude and most scrupulous exactness.

To Lund Washington, Morristown, May 19, 1780

We must do our duty in earnest, or disgrace and ruin will attend us.

To Joseph Reed, Morristown, May 28, 1780

I am resolved that no misrepresentations, falsehoods or calumny shall make me swerve from what I conceive to be the strict line of my duty.

To John Eager Howard, Philadelphia, November 30, 1795

Early Rising

Rise early, that by habit it may become familiar, agreeable, healthy, and profitable. It may for a while be irksome to do this, but that will wear off and the practice will produce a rich harvest forever thereafter.

To George Washington Parke Custis,
Mount Vernon, January 7, 1798

Education

The best means of forming a manly, virtuous, and happy people will be found in the right education of youth. Without this foundation, every other means, in my opinion, must fail.

To George Chapman, Mount Vernon, December 15, 1784

Every effort of genius and all attempts towards improving useful knowledge ought to meet with encouragement in this country.

To Nicholas Pike, Mount Vernon, June 20, 1786

In a country like this . . . if there cannot be money found to answer the common purposes of education, . . . it is evident that there is something amiss in the ruling political power.

To John Armstrong, Mount Vernon, April 25, 1788

That a national university in this country is a thing to be desired has always been my decided opinion.

To John Adams, Philadelphia, November 15, 1794

Education . . . [is] one of the surest means of enlightening and giving just ways of thinking to our citizens.

To Alexander Hamilton, Philadelphia, September 1, 1796

Elections

In all free governments, contention in elections will take place.

To Jonathan Trumbull, Philadelphia, March 3, 1797

Enemies

The most certain way to make a man your enemy is to tell him you esteem him such.

To John Banister, Valley Forge, April 21, 1778

It is at all times more easy to make enemies than friends.

To George Washington Parke Custis,
Philadelphia, November 28, 1796

Environment

How much more delightful to an undebauched mind is the task of making improvements on the earth than all the vain glory which can be acquired from ravaging it by the most uninterrupted career of conquests.

To Arthur Young, Mount Vernon, December 4, 1788

Errors

Errors once discovered are more than half amended.

To John Sullivan, New Windsor, February 4, 1781

Estate Planning

Life is always uncertain, and common prudence dictates to every man the necessity of settling his temporal concerns whilst it is in his power, and whilst the mind is calm and undisturbed.

To Martha Washington, Philadelphia, June 18, 1775

Ethics

I believe it is among nations as with individuals, the party taking advantage of the distresses of another will lose infinitely more in the opinion of mankind and in subsequent events than he will gain by the stroke of the moment.

To Gouverneur Morris, Philadelphia, July 28, 1791

Europe

We look with an anxious eye to the time ... when all Europe shall be freed from commotions, tumults, and alarms.

To Marquis de Lafayette, Philadelphia, July 28, 1791

It is the sincere wish of united America to have nothing to do with the political intrigues or the squabbles of European nations.

To the Earl of Buchan, Philadelphia, April 22, 1793

Europe has a set of primary interests, which to us have none, or a very remote relation. Hence she must be engaged in frequent controversies, the causes of which are essentially foreign to our concerns.

Farewell Address, Philadelphia, September 19, 1796

Why, by interweaving our destiny with that of any part of Europe, entangle our peace and prosperity in the toils of European ambition, rivalship, interest, humor or caprice?

Farewell Address, Philadelphia, September 19, 1796

America may think herself happy in having the Atlantic for a barrier.

To Comte de Rochambeau, Mount Vernon, December 1, 1785

Example

Example, whether it be good or bad, has a powerful influence.

To Lord Stirling, Morristown, March 5, 1780

Excuses

It is better to offer no excuse than a bad one.

To Harriet Washington, Philadelphia, October 30, 1791

Expectations

There is no truth more certain than that all our enjoyments fall short of our expectations.

To Elizabeth Parke Custis, Germantown, September 14, 1794

Experience

Experience . . . is the best rule to walk by.

To John Parke Custis, West Point, August 24, 1779

To rectify past blunders is impossible, but we might profit by the experience of them.

To Fielding Lewis, Morristown, July 6, 1780

I trust we are not too old or too proud to profit by the experience of others.

To John Jay, Mount Vernon, July 18, 1788

Extremes

To forbear running from one extreme to another is no easy matter.

To Gouverneur Morris, New York, October 13, 1789

Facial Expressions

Let your countenance be pleasant but in serious matters somewhat grave.

Rules of Civility, 1745

Faction

A fire not to be quenched, it demands a uniform vigilance to prevent its bursting into a flame, lest instead of warming it should consume.

Farewell Address, Philadelphia, September 19, 1796

False Economy

No person wishes more to save money to the public than I do, . . . but there are some cases in which parsimony may be ill placed.

To John Hancock, New York, April 23, 1776

We may spin the thread of economy 'till it breaks.

To Robert Morris, Newburgh, May 17, 1782.

Familiarity

Men who are always together get tired of each other's company.

To Thomas Jefferson, Mount Vernon, March 29, 1784

Farming

The life of a husbandman of all others is the most delectable. It is honorable, it is amusing, and, with judicious management, it is profitable.

To Alexander Spotswood, Mount Vernon, February 13, 1788

When I speak of a knowing farmer, I mean one who understands the best course of crops; how to plow, to sow, to mow, to hedge, to ditch, and above all, Midas-like, one who can convert everything he touches into manure as the first transmutation towards gold.

To George William Fairfax, Mount Vernon, June 30, 1785

Fashion

Keep to the fashion of your equals.

Rules of Civility, 1745

A person who is anxious to be a leader of the fashion, or one of the first to follow it, will certainly appear, in the eyes of judicious men, to have nothing better than a frequent change of dress to recommend him to notice.

To George Steptoe Washington,
Mount Vernon, March 23, 1789

The Federalist Papers

When the transient circumstances and fugitive performances which attended this crisis shall have disappeared, that work will merit the notice of posterity because in it are candidly and ably discussed the principles of freedom and the topics of government, which will be always interesting to mankind so long as they shall be connected in civil society.

To Alexander Hamilton, Mount Vernon, August 28, 1788

First Impressions

First impressions are generally the most lasting.

To George Steptoe Washington,
Mount Vernon, March 23, 1789

Although we cannot avoid first impressions, we may assuredly place them under guard.

To Eleanor Parke Custis, Philadelphia, January 16, 1795

Flattery

Be no flatterer.

Rules of Civility, 1745

Foreign Influence

Against the insidious wiles of foreign influence . . . the jealousy of a free people ought to be *constantly* awake.

Farewell Address, Philadelphia, September 19, 1796

Foreign Policy

It is the true policy of America not to content herself with temporary expedients, but to endeavor, if possible, to give consistency and solidity to her measures.

To Samuel Huntington, Orange Town, August 20, 1780

Separated as we are by a world of water from other nations, if we are wise we shall surely avoid being drawn into the labyrinth of their politics and involved in their destructive wars.

To Chevalier de la Luzerne, Mount Vernon, February 7, 1788

There is a rank due to the United States among nations which will be withheld, if not absolutely lost, by the reputation of weakness.

Fifth Annual Address to Congress,
Philadelphia, December 3, 1793

My policy has been, and will continue to be, . . . to be upon friendly terms with, but independent of, all the nations of the earth.

To Gouverneur Morris, Philadelphia, December 22, 1795

The great rule of conduct for us, in regard to foreign nations, is in extending our commercial relations to have with them as little political connection as possible.

Farewell Address, Philadelphia, September 19, 1796

'Tis our true policy to steer clear of permanent alliances with any portion of the foreign world.

Farewell Address, Philadelphia, September 19, 1796

We will not be dictated to by the politics of any nation under heaven.

To Alexander Hamilton, Philadelphia, May 8, 1796

Foresight

If we are wise, let us prepare for the worst.

To James McHenry, Verplanks Point, September 12, 1782

To anticipate and prevent disastrous contingencies would be the part of wisdom and patriotism.

To John Jay, Mount Vernon, August 15, 1786

Fortune

It is not uncommon ... in prosperous gales, to forget that adverse winds may blow.

To William Vans Murray, Mount Vernon, October 26, 1799

Free Trade

Our commercial policy should hold an equal and impartial hand, neither seeking nor granting exclusive favors or preferences.

Farewell Address, Philadelphia, September 19, 1796

Freedom

... a blessing on which all the good and evil of life depends.

To George Mason, Mount Vernon, April 5, 1769

My anxious recollections, my sympathetic feelings, and my best wishes are irresistibly excited whensoever, in any country, I see an oppressed nation unfurl the banners of freedom.

To Pierre Auguste Adet, Philadelphia, January 1, 1796

Freedom of Speech

In a free and republican government, you cannot restrain the voice of the multitude; every man will speak as he thinks.

To Marquis de Lafayette, White Plains, September 1, 1778

If men are to be precluded from offering their sentiments on a matter which may involve the most serious and alarming consequences, . . . the freedom of speech may be taken away and, dumb and silent, we may be led, like sheep, to the slaughter.

Address to the Officers, Newburgh, March 15, 1783

Friendship

The difference in our political sentiments never made any change in my friendship for you.

To Bryan Fairfax, Pottsgrove, September 24, 1777

A slender acquaintance with the world must convince every man that actions, not words, are the true criterion of the attachment of his friends.

To John Sullivan, Morristown, December 15, 1779

True friendship is a plant of slow growth.

To Bushrod Washington, Newburgh, January 15, 1783

The Future

I do not think we are more inspired, have more wisdom, or possess more virtue than those who will come after us.

To Bushrod Washington, Mount Vernon, November 10, 1787

Gambling

This is a vice which is productive of every possible evil, equally injurious to the morals and health of its votaries. It is the child of avarice, the brother of inequity, and father of mischief. It has been the ruin of many worthy families; the loss of many a man's honor; and the cause of suicide.

To Bushrod Washington, Newburgh, January 15, 1783

Gestures

The gestures of the body must be suited to the discourse you are upon.

Rules of Civility, 1745

God

When you speak of God or his attributes, let it be seriously and [with] reverence.

Rules of Civility, 1745

God alone is the judge of the hearts of men.

To Benedict Arnold, Cambridge, September 14, 1775

The will of heaven is not to be controverted or scrutinized by the children of this world. It therefore becomes the creatures of it to submit with patience and resignation to the will of the Creator, whether it be to prolong or to shorten the number of our days, to bless them with health, or afflict them with pain.

To George Augustine Washington,
Philadelphia, January 27, 1793

No people can be bound to acknowledge and adore the invisible hand which conducts the affairs of men more than the people of the United States.

First Inaugural Address, New York, April 30, 1789

Good and Evil

Most of the good and evil things of this life are judged of by comparison.

To Henry Laurens, Middlebrook, March 20, 1779

Good Company

Good company will always be found much less expensive than bad.

To George Steptoe Washington,
Mount Vernon, March 23, 1789

Good Humor

Good humor makes one dish of meat a feast.

Rules of Civility, 1745

Gossip

Speak not evil of the absent, for it is unjust.

Rules of Civility, 1745

Government

Influence is no government.

To Henry Lee, Mount Vernon, October 31, 1786

The aggregate happiness of the society . . . is, or ought to be, the end of all government.

To Comte de Moustier, Mount Vernon, November 1, 1790

There is no resource so firm for the government of the United States as the affections of the people guided by an enlightened policy.

*Fifth Annual Address to Congress,
Philadelphia, December 3, 1793*

Government of as much vigor as is consistent with the perfect security of liberty is indispensable.

Farewell Address, Philadelphia, September 19, 1796

The very idea of the power and the right of the people to establish government presupposes the duty of every individual to obey the established government.

Farewell Address, Philadelphia, September 19, 1796

'Tis substantially true that virtue or morality is a necessary spring of popular government.

Farewell Address, Philadelphia, September 19, 1796

Greed

Shall we at last become the victims of our own abominable lust of gain?

To James Warren, Middlebrook, March 31, 1779

Grief

'Tis time alone that can ameliorate the pangs of humanity and soften its woes.

To Henry Knox, Philadelphia, March 2, 1797

Habits

Habits are not easily taken up or suddenly laid aside.

To Marquis de Chastellux, Mount Vernon, August 18, 1786

You are now extending into that stage of life when good or bad habits are formed. When the mind will be turned to things useful and praiseworthy, or to dissipation and vice. Fix on whichever it may, it will stick by you; for you know it has been said, and truly, "that as the twig is bent, so it will grow."*

To George Washington Parke Custis,
Philadelphia, November 28, 1796.

Happiness

Happiness depends more upon the internal frame of a person's own mind than on the externals in the world.

To Mary Washington, Mount Vernon, February 15, 1787

Haste

It is easier to divert from a wrong to a right path than it is to recall the hasty and fatal steps which have been already taken.

To Joseph Jones, Newburgh, March 12, 1783

The words Washington rendered in quotation marks are paraphrased from Alexander Pope's Essay on Man (1734), which stated, "Just as the twig is bent, the tree's inclined."

Heroes and Poets

In some instances by acting reciprocally, heroes have made poets, and poets heroes.

To Marquis de Lafayette, Mount Vernon, May 28, 1788

Hindsight

We ought not to look back, unless it is to derive useful lessons from past errors, and for the purpose of profiting by dear bought experience.

To John Armstrong, New Windsor, March 26, 1781

History

Notwithstanding most of the papers which may properly be deemed official are preserved, yet the knowledge of innumerable things of a more delicate and secret nature is confined to the perishable remembrance of some few of the present generation.

To Noah Webster, Mount Vernon, July 31, 1788

Home

I should enjoy more real happiness and felicity in one month with you at home than I have the most distant prospect of reaping abroad if my stay was to be seven times seven years.

To Martha Washington, Philadelphia, June 18, 1775

Honesty

Honesty will be found, on every experiment, to be the best and only true policy.

Circular to the States, Newburgh, June 8, 1783

It is an old adage that honesty is the best policy; this applies to public as well as private life, to states as well as individuals.

To James Madison, Mount Vernon, November 30, 1785

I hope I shall always possess firmness and virtue enough to maintain (what I consider the most enviable of all titles) the character of *an honest man.*

To Alexander Hamilton, Mount Vernon, August 28, 1788

Honor

When men ... have the incitements of military honor to engage their ambition and pride, they will cheerfully submit to inconveniences which in a state of tranquillity would appear insupportable.

To Continental Congress Committee of Conference, Philadelphia, January 20, 1779

Let honor and probity be your polar star.

> To Bushrod Washington, Philadelphia, February 23, 1794

When victory, more than truth, is the palm contended for, . . . "the post of honor is a private station."*

> To Timothy Pickering, Mount Vernon, July 27, 1795

Hospitality

Virginia hospitality . . . is the most agreeable entertainment we can give, or a stranger expect to find, in an infant woody country such as ours.

> To Richard Washington, Mount Vernon, August 10, 1760

Human Nature

Men are in most cases governed first by what they feel and next by what they hope.

> To Continental Congress Committee of Conference,
> Philadelphia, January 20, 1779

We must . . . make the best of mankind as they are, since we cannot have them as we wish.

> To Philip Schuyler, Cambridge, December 24, 1775

We must take human nature as we find it.

> To John Jay, Mount Vernon, August 15, 1786

The words Washington rendered in quotation marks are from Joseph Addison's Cato (1713).

Ignorance

Ignorance and design are difficult to combat.

To John Jay, Mount Vernon, May 18, 1786

Illness

In visiting the sick, do not presently play the physician if you be not knowing therein.

Rules of Civility, 1745

Immigrants

I have established it as a maxim neither to invite nor to discourage immigrants. My opinion is that they will come hither as fast as the true interest and policy of the United States will be benefitted by foreign population.

To John Jay, Philadelphia, November 1, 1794

By an intermixture with our people, they, or their descendants, get assimilated to our customs, measures and laws: in a word, soon become one people.

To John Adams, Philadelphia, November 15, 1794

Indians

The basis of our proceedings with the Indian nations has been, and shall be justice, during the period in which I may have anything to do in the administration of this government.

To Marquis de Lafayette, New York, August 11, 1790

I cannot see much prospect of living in tranquillity with them so long as a spirit of land-jobbing prevails and our frontier settlers entertain the opinion that there is not the same crime (or indeed no crime at all) in killing an Indian as in killing a white man.

To David Humphreys, Philadelphia, July 20, 1791

Instability

The constant fluctuation of things deranges every plan as fast as adopted.

To John Hancock, Heights of Harlem, September 25, 1776

Insult

If we desire to avoid insult, we must be able to repel it.

Fifth Annual Address to Congress, Philadelphia, December 3, 1793

Integrity

Integrity and firmness is all I can promise; these, be the voyage long or short, never shall forsake me although I may be deserted by all men.

To Henry Knox, Mount Vernon, April 1, 1789

Without virtue and without integrity the finest talents and the most brilliant accomplishments can never gain the respect or conciliate the esteem of the truly valuable part of mankind.

To Bartholomew Dandridge, Philadelphia, March 8, 1797

A mind conscious of its own rectitude fears not what is said of it.

To Gouverneur Morris, Philadelphia, January 28, 1792

International Relations

It is a maxim founded on the universal experience of mankind that no nation is to be trusted farther than it is bound by its interest.

To Henry Laurens, Fredericksburg, November 14, 1778

The nation which indulges towards another an habitual hatred, or an habitual fondness, is in some degree a slave. It is a slave to its animosity or to its affection, either of which is sufficient to lead it astray from its duty and its interest.

Farewell Address, Philadelphia, September 19, 1796

'Tis folly in one nation to look for disinterested favors from another.

Farewell Address, Philadelphia, September 19, 1796

There can be no greater error than to expect or calculate upon real favors from nation to nation. 'Tis an illusion which experience must cure, which a just pride ought to discard.

Farewell Address, Philadelphia, September 19, 1796

No governments ought to interfere with the internal concerns of another except for the security of what is due to themselves.

To Marquis de Lafayette, Mount Vernon, December 25, 1798

Inventions

In whatever country useful inventions are found out and improvements made, I rejoice in contemplating that those inventions or improvements may, in some way or another, be turned to the common good of mankind.

To Comte de Moustier, Mount Vernon, December 15, 1788

Judgment

Let your judgment always balance well before you decide.

To George Washington Parke Custis,
Philadelphia, November 28, 1796

Justice

The best and only safe road to honor, glory, and true dignity is *justice*.

> To Marquis de Lafayette, West Point, September 30, 1779

Humanity will ever interfere and plead strongly against the sacrifice of an innocent person for the guilt of another.

> To Nathanael Greene, Philadelphia, December 15, 1781

Whilst we are accusing others of injustice, we should be just ourselves.

> To Bryan Fairfax, Mount Vernon, July 4, 1774

Knowledge

Do not forget that there ought to be a time appropriated to attain ... knowledge, as well as to indulge in pleasure.

> Address to the Officers, Winchester, January 8, 1756

Knowledge is in every country the surest basis of public happiness.

> First Annual Address to Congress,
> New York, January 8, 1790

Language

To be acquainted with the French tongue is become a part of polite education.

To Jonathan Boucher, Mount Vernon, January 2, 1771

To know the affinity of tongues seems to be one step towards promoting the affinity of nations.

To Marquis de Lafayette, Mount Vernon, January 10, 1788

Laws

Laws or ordinances unobserved, or partially attended to, had better never have been made.

To James Madison, Mount Vernon, March 31, 1787

If the laws are to be so trampled upon with impunity, . . . there is an end put at one stroke to republican government, and nothing but anarchy and confusion is to be expected thereafter; for some other man or society may dislike another law and oppose it with equal propriety until all laws are prostrate, and everyone . . . will carve for himself.

To Charles Mynn Thruston, Philadelphia, August 10, 1794

There never was a law yet made, I conceive, that hit the taste exactly of every man or every part of the community.

To Daniel Morgan, Carlisle, October 8, 1794

Lawsuits

Of all the vexations in life, that of a tedious and perplexing lawsuit is the most disagreeable.

To Edward Newenham, February 24, 1788

Leadership

Unanimity in our councils, disinterestedness in our pursuits, and steady perseverance in our national duty are the only means to avoid misfortunes.

To Thomas Nelson, Middlebrook, March 16, 1779

So much prudence, so much perseverance, so much disinterestedness, and so much patriotism are necessary among the leaders of a nation in order to promote the national felicity that sometimes my fears nearly preponderate over my expectations.

To Marquis de la Luzerne, New York, April 29, 1790

Men in responsible situations cannot, like those in private life, be governed solely by the dictates of their own inclinations, or by such motives as can only affect themselves.

To Duc de la Rochefoucauld-Liancourt,
Mount Vernon, August 8, 1796

Liberty

The cause of virtue and liberty is confined to no continent or climate; it comprehends within its capacious limits the wise and the good, however dispersed and separated in space or distance.

To the Inhabitants of Bermuda, Cambridge, September 6, 1775

Liberty, when it begins to take root, is a plant of rapid growth.

To James Madison, Mount Vernon, March 2, 1788

The preservation of the sacred fire of liberty and the destiny of the republican model of government are justly considered as *deeply*, perhaps as *finally*, staked on the experiment entrusted to the hands of the American people.

First Inaugural Address, New York, April 30, 1789

While we are contending for our own liberty, we should be very cautious of violating the rights of conscience in others.

To Benedict Arnold, Cambridge, September 14, 1775

Love

Like all things else, when nourished and supplied plentifully with aliment, it is rapid in its progress; but let these be withdrawn and it may be stifled in its birth or much stinted in its growth.

To Eleanor Parke Custis, Philadelphia, January 16, 1795

No distance can keep anxious lovers long asunder.

To Marquis de Lafayette, West Point, September 30, 1779

Love is too dainty a food to live upon *alone.*

To Elizabeth Parke Custis, Germantown, September 14, 1794

Marriage

I have always considered marriage as the most interesting event of one's life, the foundation of happiness or misery.

To Burwell Bassett, Mount Vernon, May 23, 1785

In my estimation, more permanent and genuine happiness is to be found in the sequestered walks of connubial life than in the giddy rounds of promiscuous pleasure.

To Charles Armand-Tuffin, Mount Vernon, August 10, 1786

Do not then in your contemplation of the marriage state look for perfect felicity before you consent to wed. Nor conceive, from the fine tales the poets and lovers of old have told us of the transports of mutual love, that heaven has taken its abode on earth.

To Elizabeth Parke Custis, Germantown, September 14, 1794

Mathematics

Without arithmetic, the common affairs of life are not to be managed with success.

To Jonathan Boucher, Mount Vernon, January 2, 1771

The investigation of mathematical truths accustoms the mind to method and correctness in reasoning, and is an employment peculiarly worthy of rational beings.

To Nicholas Pike, Mount Vernon, June 20, 1788

The science of figures, to a certain degree, is . . . indispensably requisite in every walk of civilized life.

To Nicholas Pike, Mount Vernon, June 20, 1788

Men and Women

Men and women feel the same inclinations to each other now that they always have done, and which they will continue to do until there is a new order of things.

To Eleanor Parke Custis, Philadelphia, January 16, 1795

Once the woman has tempted us and we have tasted the forbidden fruit, there is no such thing as checking our appetites, whatever the consequences may be.

To Annis Boudinot Stockton, Rocky Hill, September 2, 1783

Mercenaries

A freeman contending for liberty on his own ground is superior to any slavish mercenary on earth.

General Orders, New York, July 2, 1776

Merit

Reward and punish every man according to his merit, without partiality or prejudice.

To William Woodford, Cambridge, November 10, 1775

Merit rarely goes unrewarded.

To Bushrod Washington, Newburgh, January 15, 1783

Military Establishments

Avoid the necessity of those overgrown military establishments, which under any form of government are inauspicious to liberty and which are to be regarded as particularly hostile to republican liberty.

Farewell Address, Philadelphia, September 19, 1796

Military Orders

Orders, unless they are followed by close attention to the performance of them, are of little avail. They are read by some, only heard of by others, and inaccurately attended to by all.

To Lord Stirling, Morristown, March 5, 1780

A refusal to obey the commands of a superior officer, especially where the duty required was evidently calculated for the good of the service, cannot be justified without involving consequences subversive of all military discipline.

To Josias Carvil Hall, Valley Forge, April 3, 1778

Military Rank

The consequence of giving rank indiscriminately is much to be dreaded. . . . The too great liberality practiced in this respect will destroy the pride of rank where it ought to exist, and will not only render it cheap but contemptible.

To a Committee of the Continental Congress,
Camp at the Clove, July 19, 1777

Military Science

A thorough examination of the subject will evince that the art of war is at once comprehensive and complicated;

that it demands much previous study; and that the possession of it, in its most improved and perfect state, is always of great moment to the security of a nation.

Eighth Annual Address to Congress,
Philadelphia, December 7, 1796

Millennialism

Mankind are not yet ripe for the millennial state.

To Edward Newenham, Mount Vernon, August 29, 1788

Misfortune

Show not yourself glad at the misfortune of another though he were your enemy.

Rules of Civility, 1745

It is our duty to make the best of our misfortunes.

To William Heath, White Plains, August 28, 1778

Misinformation

Concealment is a species of misinformation.

To Timothy Pickering, Mount Vernon, February 10, 1799

Monarchy

It is a wonder to me there should be found a single monarch who does not realize that his own glory and felicity must depend on the prosperity and happiness of his people.

To Marquis de Lafayette, Mount Vernon, June 19, 1788

Money

The friends of the measure are better stocked with good wishes than money, the former of which unfortunately goes but a little way in works where the latter is necessary.

To Thomas Jefferson, Mount Vernon, February 25, 1785

Money, we know, will fetch anything and command the services of any man.

To George William Fairfax, Mount Vernon, June 30, 1785

Money and Politics

It would be repugnant to the vital principles of our government virtually to exclude from public trusts [people with] talents and virtue unless accompanied by wealth.

Eighth Annual Address to Congress,
Philadelphia, December 7, 1796

Morality

Purity of morals ... [is] the only sure foundation of public happiness in any country.

General Orders, Fredericksburg, October 21, 1778

The propitious smiles of Heaven can never be expected on a nation that disregards the eternal rules of order and right which Heaven itself has ordained.

First Inaugural Address, New York, April 30, 1789

Let us with caution indulge the supposition that morality can be maintained without religion.

Farewell Address, Philadelphia, September 19, 1796

Motives

There is scarcely any action whose motives may not be subject to a double interpretation.

To Catherine Macaulay Graham, New York, January 9, 1790

Mount Vernon

I can truly say I had rather be at Mount Vernon with a friend or two about me than to be attended at the seat of government by the officers of state and the representatives of every power in Europe.

To David Stuart, New York, June 15, 1790

National Debt

No pecuniary consideration is more urgent than the regular redemption and discharge of the public debt.

Fifth Annual Address to Congress,
Philadelphia, December 3, 1793

As far as may be practicable, we ought to . . . prevent that progressive accumulation of debt which must ultimately endanger all governments.

Sixth Annual Address to Congress,
Philadelphia, November 19, 1794

National Service

Every citizen who enjoys the protection of a free government owes not only a proportion of his property, but even of his personal services to the defense of it.

Sentiments on a Peace Establishment, Newburgh, May 2, 1783

Every man who is in the vigor of life ought to serve his country in whatsoever line it requires and he is fit for.

To David Humphreys, Mount Vernon, June 26, 1797

Nature

Nature, however she may be opposed for a while, will soon return [to] her regular course.

To Thomas Jefferson, Philadelphia, May 30, 1787

Navy

No land force can act decisively unless it is accompanied by a maritime superiority.

To Marquis de Lafayette, Mount Vernon, November 15, 1781

Negotiations

To enter into a negotiation too hastily, or to reject it altogether, may be attended with consequences equally fatal.

To John Banister, Valley Forge, April 21, 1778

It is hardly possible in the early stages of a negotiation to foresee all the results, so much depending upon fortuitous circumstances and incidents which are not within our control.

To John Jay, Philadelphia, November 1, 1794

The nature of foreign negotiations requires caution, and their success must often depend on secrecy.

To the House of Representatives, Philadelphia, March 30, 1796

Obedience

The person commanded yields but a reluctant obedience to those he conceives are undeservedly made his superiors.

To Patrick Henry, Heights of Harlem, October 5, 1776

Officers

Remember that it is the actions, and not the commission, that make the officer—and that there is more expected from him than the title.

Address to the Officers, Winchester, January 8, 1756

The true distinction ... between what is called a fine regiment and an indifferent one will ever, upon investigation, be found to originate in and depend upon the care, or the inattention, of the officers.

To Thomas Lansdale, Newburgh, January 25, 1783

An army cannot exist without officers.

To Continental Congress Committee of Conference, Philadelphia, January 20, 1779

Opinions

So various are the tastes, opinions and whims of men that even the sanction of divinity does not ensure universal concurrence.

To Francis Hopkinson, Mount Vernon, February 5, 1789

Where there is no occasion for expressing an opinion, it is best to be silent.

To George Washington Parke Custis, Philadelphia, November 28, 1796

To give opinions unsupported by reasons might appear dogmatical.

To Alexander Spotswood, Philadelphia, November 22, 1798

Opponents

It ever has been that the adversaries to a measure are more active than its friends.

To Bushrod Washington, Mount Vernon, November 10, 1787

Optimism

I flatter myself that a superintending Providence is ordering everything for the best and that, in due time, all will end well.

To Landon Carter, Philadelphia County, October 27, 1777

I have no doubt but that everything happens so for the best; that we shall triumph over all our misfortunes and shall, in the end, be ultimately happy.

To Marquis de Lafayette, Valley Forge, December 31, 1777

Passions

In the composition of the human frame there is a good deal of inflammable matter, however dormant it may lie for a time, and . . . when the torch is put to it, that which is within you may burst into a blaze.

To Eleanor Parke Custis, Philadelphia, January 16, 1795

In all causes of passion admit reason to govern.

Rules of Civility, 1745

Patience

Patience is a noble virtue, and when rightly exercised does not fail of its reward.

To John Rodgers, Newburgh, June 11, 1783

Patriotism

I was summoned by my country, whose voice I can never hear but with veneration and love.

First Inaugural Address, New York, April 30, 1789

The welfare of our country is the great object to which our cares and efforts ought to be directed.

To the Senate and the House of Representatives,
New York, January 8, 1790

I have no wish superior to that of promoting the happiness and welfare of this country.

To Henry Lee, Philadelphia, July 21, 1793

If real danger threatened the country, no young man ought to be an idle spectator of its defense.

To David Stuart, Mount Vernon, December 30, 1798

I do not mean to exclude altogether the idea of patriotism. I know it exists, and I know it has done much in the present contest. But I will venture to assert that a great and lasting war can never be supported on this principle alone. It must be aided by a prospect of interest or some reward. For a time, it may, of itself, push men to action, to bear much, to encounter difficulties, but it will not endure unassisted by interest.

To John Banister, Valley Forge, April 21, 1778

Peace

Men are naturally fond of peace.

To John Banister, Valley Forge, April 21, 1778

My first wish is . . . to see the whole world in peace and the inhabitants of it as one band of brothers, striving who should contribute most to the happiness of mankind.

To Charles Armand-Tuffin, Mount Vernon, October 7, 1785

Peace with all the world is my sincere wish.

To Jonathan Boucher, Mount Vernon, August 15, 1798

If we desire to secure peace, . . . it must be known that we are at all times ready for war.

Fifth Annual Address to Congress,
Philadelphia, December 3, 1793

Perfection

Perfection falls not to the share of mortals.

To John Jay, Mount Vernon, August 15, 1786

We are not to expect perfection in this world.

To Marquis de Lafayette, Mount Vernon, February 7, 1788

Perseverance

Perseverance and spirit have done wonders in all ages.

To Philip Schuyler, Cambridge, August 20, 1775

Personal Experience

The experience of others is not attended to as it ought to be; we must *feel ourselves* before we can think or perceive the danger that threatens.

To John Marshall, Mount Vernon, December 4, 1797

Personal Faults

I shall never attempt to palliate my own faults by exposing those of another.

To Joseph Reed, West Point, August 22, 1779

Perspective

A bystander sees more of the game, generally, than those who are playing it.

To William Vans Murray, Mount Vernon, October 26, 1799

Pessimism

Human affairs are always checkered, and vicissitudes in this life are rather to be expected than wondered at.

To Robert Stewart, Williamsburg, April 27, 1763

Life and the concerns of this world, one would think, are so uncertain, and so full of disappointments, that nothing is to be counted upon from human actions.

To Henry Lee, Mount Vernon, July 26, 1786

It is in vain, I perceive, to look for ease and happiness in a world of troubles.

To Henry Knox, Mount Vernon, July 16, 1798

Pleasing Other People

To please everybody is impossible; were I to undertake it, I should probably please nobody.

To John Armstrong, Middlebrook, May 18, 1779

Plundering

How many noble designs have miscarried, how many victories been lost, how many armies ruined by an indulgence of soldiers in plundering?

General Orders, Wilmington, September 4, 1777

Poetry

Fiction is to be sure the very life and soul of poetry.

To Annis Boudinot Stockton, Rocky Hill, September 2, 1783

Politics

The best way to preserve the confidence of the people durably is to promote their true interest.

To Joseph Reed, Preakness, July 4, 1780

A difference of opinion on political points is not to be imputed to freemen as a fault, since it is to be presumed that they are all actuated by an equally laudable and sacred regard for the liberties of their country.

To the Governor and Council of North Carolina,
New York, June 19, 1789

All see, and most admire, the glare which hovers round the external trappings of elevated office.

To Catharine Macaulay Graham, New York, January 9, 1790

To expect that all men should think alike upon political, more than on religious or other subjects, would be to look for a change in the order of nature.

To Joseph Hopkinson, Mount Vernon, May 27, 1798

Popularity

I would not seek or retain popularity at the expense of one social duty or moral virtue.

To Henry Lee, Mount Vernon, September 22, 1788

Positive Thinking

It is assuredly better to go laughing than crying through the rough journey of life.

To Theodorick Bland, Mount Vernon, August 15, 1786

Potatoes

Of all the improving and ameliorating crops, none, in my opinion, is equal to potatoes.

To Thomas Jefferson, Mount Vernon, October 4, 1795

Power

I have no lust after power.

To John Hancock, Trenton Falls, December 20, 1776

Arbitrary power is most easily established on the ruins of liberty abused to licentiousness.

Circular to the States, Newburgh, June 8, 1783

Experience has taught us that men will not adopt and carry into execution measures the best calculated for their own good without the intervention of a coercive power.

To John Jay, Mount Vernon, August 15, 1786

Precedents

Precedents are dangerous things.

To Henry Lee, Mount Vernon, October 31, 1786

If it operates as a bad precedent, we must endeavor to correct it when we have it in our power.

To Continental Congress Committee of Conference,
Philadelphia, January 20, 1779

Preparedness

Being in a state of perfect preparation for war is the only sure and infallible means of producing peace.

To John Mitchell, Verplanks Point, September 16, 1782

It will always be wise for America to be prepared for events.

To Jonathan Trumbull, Mount Vernon, July 20, 1788

Timely disbursements to prepare for danger frequently prevent much greater disbursements to repel it.

Farewell Address, Philadelphia, September 19, 1796

The Presidency

The presidency . . . has no enticing charms and no fascinating allurements for me.

To Marquis de Lafayette, Mount Vernon, April 28, 1788

Whilst I am in office, I shall never suffer private convenience to interfere with what I conceive to be my official duties.

To Edmund Randolph, Mount Vernon, July 29, 1795

The executive branch of this government never has, nor will suffer, while I preside, any improper conduct of its officers to escape with impunity.

To Gouverneur Morris, Philadelphia, December 22, 1795

The Press

I consider such easy vehicles of knowledge [newspapers and magazines] more happily calculated than any other to preserve the liberty, stimulate the industry, and meliorate the morals of an enlightened and free people.

To Mathew Carey, Mount Vernon, June 25, 1788

If the government and the officers of it are to be the constant theme for newspaper abuse, ... it will be impossible, I conceive, for any man living to manage the helm or to keep the machine together.

To Edmund Randolph, Mount Vernon, August 26, 1792

We get so many details in the gazettes, and of such different complexions, that it is impossible to know what credence to give to any of them.

To James McHenry, Mount Vernon, April 3, 1797

Prevention

It is easier to prevent than to remedy an evil.

To Richard Henry Lee, Mount Vernon, December 14, 1784

Price Controls

To limit the prices of articles ... is inconsistent with the very nature of things and impracticable in itself.

To James Warren, Middlebrook, March 31, 1779

Procrastination

The habit of postponing things is among the worst in the world.

To Howell Lewis, Germantown, November 3, 1793

Promises

Undertake not what you cannot perform, but be careful to keep your promise.

Rules of Civility, 1745

I never wish to promise more than I have a moral certainty of performing.

To Marquis de Lafayette, Preakness, July 16, 1780

Promotion

Let your promotion result from your own application and from intrinsic merit, not from the labors of others.

To George Washington Parke Custis,
Philadelphia, November 15, 1796

Public Service

Every post is honorable in which a man can serve his country.

To Benedict Arnold, Cambridge, September 14, 1775

The consciousness of having discharged that duty which we owe to our country is superior to all other considerations.

To James Madison, Mount Vernon, March 2, 1788

My whole life has been dedicated to the service of my country in one shape or another.

To James McHenry, Mount Vernon, July 4, 1798

Public Speaking

Speak seldom, but to important subjects, except such as particularly relate to your constituents, and, in the former case, make yourself perfectly master of the subject.

To Bushrod Washington, Mount Vernon, November 10, 1787

Reading

Light reading (by this, I mean books of little importance) may amuse for the moment but leaves nothing solid behind.

To George Washington Parke Custis,
Philadelphia, December 19, 1796

Reason

There is reason in all things.

To Marquis de Lafayette, West Point, September 30, 1779

Regrets

I will not repine—I have had my day.

To Marquis de Lafayette, Mount Vernon, December 8, 1784

Religion

While we are zealously performing the duties of good citizens and soldiers, we certainly ought not to be inattentive to the higher duties of religion.

General Orders, Valley Forge, May 2, 1778

Religion and morality are the essential pillars of civil society.

To the Clergy of Different Denominations,
Philadelphia, March 3, 1797

Religious Disputes

Religious controversies are always productive of more acrimony and irreconcilable hatreds than those which spring from any other cause.

To Edward Newenham, Philadelphia, June 22, 1792

Of all the animosities which have existed among mankind, those which are caused by a difference of sentiments in religion appear to be the most inveterate and distressing, and ought most to be deprecated.

To Edward Newenham, Philadelphia, October 20, 1792

Religious Freedom

No man's sentiments are more opposed to *any kind* of restraint upon religious principles than mine are.

To George Mason, Mount Vernon, October 3, 1785

Every man, conducting himself as a good citizen and being accountable to God alone for his religious opinions, ought to be protected in worshipping the Deity according to the dictates of his own conscience.

To the United Baptist Churches of Virginia,
New York, May 1789

The liberty enjoyed by the people of these states of worshipping almighty God agreeable to their consciences is not only among the choicest of their blessings, but also of their rights.

To the Society of Quakers, New York, September 28, 1789

The government of the United States, which gives to bigotry no sanction, to persecution no assistance, requires only that they who live under its protection should demean themselves as good citizens in giving it on all occasions their effectual support.

To the Hebrew Congregation, Newport, August 18, 1790

In this land of equal liberty it is our boast that a man's religious tenets will not forfeit the protection of the laws nor deprive him of the right of attaining and holding the highest offices that are known in the United States.

To Members of the New Church in Baltimore,
Philadelphia, January 27, 1793

Remedies

Desperate diseases require desperate remedies.

To John Hancock, Trenton Falls, December 20, 1776

Remodeling

Workmen in most countries, I believe, are necessary plagues; in this, where entreaties as well as money must be used to obtain their work and keep them to their duty, they baffle all calculation in the accomplishment of any plan or repairs they are engaged in and require more attention to, and looking after, than can well be conceived.

To William Gordon, Mount Vernon, October 15, 1797

Representatives

Representatives ought to be the mouth of their constituents.

To Bushrod Washington, Mount Vernon, November 15, 1786

Reproach

Wherein you reprove another, be unblamable yourself.

Rules of Civility, 1745

Reproach none for the infirmities of nature.

Rules of Civility, 1745

Republican Form of Government

Under no form of government will laws be better supported, liberty and property better secured, or happiness be more effectually dispensed to mankind.

To Edmund Pendleton, Philadelphia, January 22, 1795

Reputation

Reputation derives it[s] principal support from success.

To Burwell Bassett, Philadelphia, June 19, 1775

To stand well in the good opinion of my countrymen constitutes my chiefest happiness.

To Benjamin Harrison, Middlebrook, December 18, 1778

To merit the approbation of good and virtuous men is the height of my ambition.

To Thomas Jefferson, Newburgh, February 10, 1783

The good opinion of honest men, friends to freedom and well-wishers to mankind, wherever they may be born or happen to reside, is the only kind of reputation a wise man would ever desire.

To Edward Pemberton, Mount Vernon, June 20, 1788

Respect

Every action done in company ought to be with some sign of respect to those that are present.

Rules of Civility, 1745

Retaliation

Retaliation is certainly just and sometimes necessary, even where attended with the severest penalties. But when the evils which may and must result from it exceed those intended to be redressed, prudence and policy require that it should be avoided.

To John Hancock, Morristown, March 1, 1777

Retirement

I am not only retired from all public employments, but I am retiring within myself and shall be able to view the solitary walk and tread the paths of private life with heartfelt satisfaction. Envious of none, I am determined to be pleased with all.

To Marquis de Lafayette, Mount Vernon, February 1, 1784

I . . . look forward to the fulfillment of my fondest and most ardent wishes to spend the remainder of my days (which I cannot expect will be many) in ease and tranquillity.

To James Madison, Mount Vernon, May 20, 1792

No man was ever more tired of public life, or more devoutly wished for retirement, than I do.

To Edmund Pendleton, Philadelphia, January 22, 1795

Every day the increasing weight of years admonishes me more and more that the shade of retirement is as necessary to me as it will be welcome.

Farewell Address, Philadelphia, September 19, 1796

Revolutions

The rapidity of national revolutions appear no less astonishing than their magnitude.

To David Humphreys, Philadelphia, March 23, 1793

Standing, as it were, in the midst of falling empires, it should be our aim to assume a station and attitude which will preserve us from being overwhelmed in their ruins.

To James McHenry, Philadelphia, December 13, 1798

Ridicule

Ridicule . . . begets enmity not easy to be forgotten.

To Gouverneur Morris, Philadelphia, January 28, 1792

Rum

Rum . . . is, in my opinion, the bane of morals and the parent of idleness.

To Comte de Moustier, Mount Vernon, December 15, 1788

Rumors

Be not apt to relate news if you know not the truth thereof.

Rules of Civility, 1745

Be not hasty to believe flying reports to the disparagement of any.

Rules of Civility, 1745

Science

There is nothing which can better deserve your patronage than the promotion of science and literature.

First Annual Address to Congress,
New York, January 8, 1790

Secrecy

What you may speak in secret to your friend deliver not before others.

Rules of Civility, 1745

Secrecy and dispatch must prove the soul of success to enterprise.

To David Cobb, near Peekskill, June 30, 1781

Self-Interest

A small knowledge of human nature will convince us that, with far the greatest part of mankind, interest is the governing principle and that almost every man is more or less under its influence.

To Continental Congress Committee of Conference,
Valley Forge, January 29, 1778

Few men are capable of making a continual sacrifice of all views of private interest, or advantage, to the common good.

To Continental Congress Committee of Conference,
Valley Forge, January 29, 1778

Sermons

I went to hear morning service performed in the Dutch reformed church—which being in that language, not a word of which I understood, I was in no danger of becoming a proselyte to its religion by the eloquence of the preacher.

Diary entry, York, July 3, 1791

Silence

Silence . . . in some cases . . . speaks more intelligibly than the sweetest eloquence.

To Sarah Cary (Sally) Fairfax,
Fort Cumberland, September 12, 1758

Sincerity

My feelings will not permit me to make professions of friendship to the man I deem my enemy.

To Henry Laurens, Valley Forge, January 2, 1778

I never say anything of a man that I have the smallest scruple of saying to him.

To Robert Morris, Newburgh, June 16, 1782

Sitting for Portraits

At first I was as impatient at the request, and as restive under the operation, as a colt is of the saddle. The next time I submitted very reluctantly, but with less flouncing. Now no dray moves more readily to the thill than I do to the painter's chair.

To Francis Hopkinson, Mount Vernon, May 16, 1785

Slander

To persevere in one's duty and be silent is the best answer to calumny.

To William Livingston, Morristown, December 7, 1779

The best way therefore to disconcert and defeat them [slanderers] is to take no notice of their publications.

To Samuel Vaughan, Mount Vernon, November 30, 1785

Slavery

There is not a man living who wishes more sincerely than I do, to see a plan adopted for the abolition of it.

To Robert Morris, Mount Vernon, April 12, 1786

I never mean . . . to possess another slave by purchase, it being among my first wishes to see some plan adopted by the legislature, by which slavery in this country may be abolished by slow, sure, and imperceptible degrees.

To John Francis Mercer, Mount Vernon, September 9, 1786

I wish from my soul that the legislature of this state [Virginia] could see the policy of a gradual abolition of slavery.

To Lawrence Lewis, Mount Vernon, August 4, 1797

The Soldier-Citizen

When we assumed the soldier, we did not lay aside the citizen, and we shall most sincerely rejoice with you in that happy hour when the establishment of American liberty, on the most firm and solid foundations, shall enable us to return to our private stations in the bosom of a free, peaceful, and happy country.

To the New York Provincial Congress, New York, June 26, 1775,
shortly after assuming command of the American army

Soldiers and Politicians

It is a much easier and less distressing thing to draw remonstrances in a comfortable room by a good fireside than to occupy a cold, bleak hill and sleep under frost and snow without clothes or blankets.

To Henry Laurens, Valley Forge, December 23, 1777

Speech

Think before you speak; pronounce not imperfectly, nor bring out your words too hastily, but orderly and distinctly.

Rules of Civility, 1745

Never exceed a decent warmth, and submit your sentiments with diffidence. A dictatorial style, though it may carry conviction, is always accompanied with disgust.

To Bushrod Washington, Mount Vernon, November 10, 1787

My words are few and plain; but I will make good what I say.

Speech to the Delaware Chiefs, Middlebrook, May 12, 1779

Spies

Single men in the night will be more likely to ascertain facts than the best glasses in the day.

To Anthony Wayne, New Windsor, July 10, 1779

Strategy

We should on all occasions avoid a general action or put anything to the risk unless compelled by a necessity, into which we ought never to be drawn.

To John Hancock, New York, September 8, 1776

We must not despair; the game is yet in our own hands; to play it well is all we have to do.

To John Mathews, New Windsor, June 7, 1781

Frequently the most effectual way to defend is to attack.

To James McHenry, Philadelphia, December 13, 1798

Stress

A mind that has been constantly on the stretch . . . with but short intervals, and little relaxation, requires rest and composure.

To Jonathan Trumbull, Mount Vernon, August 30, 1799

Success

We cannot, by the best concerted plans, absolutely command success.

Circular to the States, Philadelphia, January 31, 1782

Suspicions

Suspicions unfounded, and jealousies too lively, are irritating to honest feelings and oftentimes are productive of more evil than good.

To James Madison, Mount Vernon, May 20, 1792

System

System in all things should be aimed at, for in execution it renders everything more easy.

To George Washington Parke Custis,
Mount Vernon, January 7, 1798

Taxes

No taxes can be devised which are not more or less inconvenient and unpleasant.

Farewell Address, Philadelphia, September 19, 1796

Teamwork

A hundred thousand men, coming one after another, cannot move a ton weight, but the united strength of fifty would transport it with ease.

To William Gordon, Newburgh, July 8, 1783

It is infinitely better to have a few good men than many indifferent ones.

To James McHenry, Mount Vernon, August 10, 1798

Tedium

Be not tedious in discourse or in reading unless you find the company pleased therewith.

Rules of Civility, 1745

Thought and Action

From thinking proceeds speaking, thence to acting is often but a single step. But how irrevocable and tremendous!

To John Jay, Mount Vernon, August 15, 1786

Time

Time *alone* can blunt the keen edge of afflictions.

To Benjamin Lincoln, Mount Vernon, February 11, 1788

Time may unfold more than prudence ought to disclose.

To Henry Lee, Philadelphia, July 21, 1793

The man who does not estimate time as money will forever miscalculate.

To James Anderson, Mount Vernon, December 21, 1797

Future years cannot compensate for lost days.

*To George Steptoe Washington,
Philadelphia, December 5, 1790*

Every hour misspent is lost forever.

To George Steptoe Washington,
Philadelphia, December 5, 1790

Toleration

All those who conduct themselves as worthy members of the community are equally entitled to the protection of civil government. I hope ever to see America among the foremost nations in examples of justice and liberality.

To the Roman Catholics in the United States,
New York, March 1790

Treason

No punishment, in my opinion, is too great for the man who can build his greatness upon his country's ruin.

To Joseph Reed, Middlebrook, December 12, 1778

Traitors are the growth of every country.

To Comte de Rochambeau,
Near West Point, September 26, 1780

Treaties

Treaties which are not built upon reciprocal benefits are not likely to be of long duration.

To Comte de Moustier, Mount Vernon, March 26, 1788

All treaties and compacts formed by the United States with other nations . . . should be made with caution and executed with fidelity.

To the United States Senate, New York, September 17, 1789

Truth

Truth is not always related without embellishment.

To David Stuart, New York, July 29, 1789

Truth will ultimately prevail where pains is taken to bring it to light.

To Charles Mynn Thruston, Philadelphia, August 10, 1794

There is but one straight course, and that is to seek truth and pursue it steadily.

To Edmund Randolph, Mount Vernon, July 31, 1795

What can be so proper as the truth?

To Richard Washington, Fort Loudoun, April 15, 1757

Turbulent Times

In times of turbulence, when the passions are afloat, calm reason is swallowed up.

To John Luzac, Mount Vernon, December 2, 1797

U.S. Constitution

It approached nearer to perfection than any government hitherto instituted among men.

To Edward Newenham, Mount Vernon, August 29, 1788

The Constitution is the guide which I never will abandon.

To the Boston Selectmen, Mount Vernon, July 28, 1795

The power under the Constitution will always be in the people.

To Bushrod Washington,
Mount Vernon, November 10, 1787

The basis of our political systems is the right of the people to make and alter their constitutions of government. But the constitution which at any time exists, 'till changed by an explicit and authentic act of the whole people, is sacredly obligatory upon all.

Farewell Address, Philadelphia, September 19, 1796

Valley Forge

No history now extant can furnish an instance of an army's suffering such uncommon hardships as ours have done and bearing them with the same patience and fortitude. To see men without clothes to cover their nakedness, without blankets to lay on, without shoes, by which their marches might be traced by the blood from their feet, and almost as often without provisions as with, marching through frost and snow and at Christmas taking up their winter quarters within a day's march of the enemy without a house or hut to cover them till they could be built, and submitting to it without a murmur, is a mark of patience and obedience which in my opinion can scarce be paralleled.

To John Banister, Valley Forge, April 21, 1778

Values

Men set different values upon the same thing according to the lights in which it strikes them.

To Benjamin Dulany, Mount Vernon, November 17, 1781

Vanity

There is no restraining men's tongues, or pens, when charged with a little vanity.

To Joseph Reed, Cambridge, December 15, 1775

Vinegar

Rum should compose no part of a soldier's ration; but vinegar in large quantities should be issued.

Sentiments on a Peace Establishment,
Newburgh, May 2, 1783

Virtue

There is no truth more thoroughly established than that there exists in the economy and course of nature an indissoluble union between virtue and happiness.

First Inaugural Address, New York, April 30, 1789

Few men have virtue to withstand the highest bidder.

To Robert Howe, West Point, August 17, 1779

Wants

Imaginary wants are indefinite and oftentimes insatiable, because they are boundless and always changing.

To John Augustine Washington,
Newburgh, January 16, 1783

War

In modern wars the longest purse must chiefly determine the event.

To Joseph Reed, Morristown, May 28, 1780

My first wish is to see this plague to mankind banished from off the earth.

To David Humphreys, Mount Vernon, July 25, 1785

In the game of war, there are so many contingencies that often prevent the most probable events from taking place.

To Edward Newenham, Mount Vernon, August 29, 1788

The friends of humanity will deprecate war wheresoever it may appear.

To the Merchants and Traders of the City of Philadelphia,
Philadelphia, May 17, 1793

Nothing short of self respect and that justice which is essential to a national character ought to involve us in war.

To Gouverneur Morris, Philadelphia, December 22, 1795

The vicissitudes of war are not within the reach of human control.

To James McHenry, Mount Vernon, July 4, 1798

It is really a strange thing that there should not be room enough in the world for men to live without cutting one another's throats.

To Marquis de Lafayette, Mount Vernon, June 19, 1788

The globe is large enough; why, then, need we wrangle for a small spot of it?

To Marquis de Chastellux, Mount Vernon, September 5, 1785

Winter Campaigns

In general, winter campaigns are destructive to troops, and nothing but pressing necessity and the best state of preparation can justify them.

To Philip Schuyler, Fredericksburg, November 20, 1778

Wisdom

To inveigh against things that are past and irremediable is unpleasing; but to steer clear of the shelves and rocks we have struck upon is the part of wisdom.

To John Armstrong, New Windsor, March 26, 1781

If we cannot learn wisdom from experience, it is hard to say where it is to be found.

To Bushrod Washington, Mount Vernon, November 10, 1787

Women

I never did, nor do I believe I ever shall give advice to a woman who is setting out on a matrimonial voyage. . . . A woman very rarely asks an opinion or requires advice on such an occasion 'till her resolution is formed.

To Lund Washington, Rocky Hill, September 20, 1783

Nothing short of good sense and an easy unaffected conduct can draw the line between prudery and coquetry.

To Eleanor Parke Custis, Philadelphia, January 16, 1795

You, as others have done, may find, perhaps, that the passions of your sex are easier raised than allayed. Do not therefore boast too soon or too smugly of your insensibility to, or resistance of, its powers.

To Eleanor Parke Custis, Philadelphia, January 16, 1795

A sensible woman can never be happy with a fool.

To Eleanor Parke Custis, Philadelphia, January 16, 1795

Writing

Composition, like other things, is made more perfect by practice and attention and just criticism thereon.

To George Washington Parke Custis,
Mount Vernon, July 23, 1797

All of his writing that I have seen is a hurried scribble, as if to get to the end speedily was the sole object of writing.

To John McDowell, Mount Vernon, September 2, 1798,
referring to George Washington Parke Custis,
stepgrandson of George Washington

Zeal

Too much zeal may create suspicion.

To Henry Lee, Preakness, October 20, 1780

INDEX

Lincoln, Benjamin, 94
literature, 9, 87
Livingston, Robert R., 3
Livingston, William, 89
love, 55–56
lovers, 56
Luzac, John, 96
Luzerne, Chevalier de la, 36
Luzerne, Marquis de la, 54

Madison, James, vii, xi, xii, 13, 16,
    46, 53, 55, 79, 85, 92
magazines, 75
Malmedy, Marquis de, 23
manure, 34
marriage, 56, 101, 102
Marshall, John, 69
Marsteller, Philip, 10
Mason, George, 38, 81
mastery of the subject, 79
mathematics, 57
Mathews, John, 92
maxims, ix, 11, 48, 50. *See also* truths
McDowell, John, 102
McHenry, James, xi, 37, 75, 79, 86,
    92, 93, 100
medical advice, 48
men and women, 57, 101–2
mercenaries, 58
Mercer, John Francis, 90
Merchants and Traders of the City
    of Philadelphia, 100
merit, 58, 61, 76
military establishments, 58
military honor, 46
military officers, 65
military orders, 59. *See also* obedience
military rank, 59
military science, 59–60
millennialism, 60
misfortune, 54, 60, 66
misinformation, 60
mistakes, 32, 45. *See also* errors
Mitchell, John, 74
mob, 8
modesty, 8, 15
monarchy, 61
money, 61; borrowing, 12; and edu-
    cation, 29; and politics, 61; and
    time, 94; and war, 99. *See also*
    bargains; business; commerce;
    estate planning; false economy;
    free trade; national debt; price
    controls; public credit; taxes
Moore, Charles, xiv
morality, 40, 62, 75, 86; and civil society, 62, 80; and government,
    43; and religion, 62; and popu-
    larity, 72. *See also* character;
    ethics; honor; integrity; virtue
Morgan, Daniel, 53
Morris, Gouverneur, 18, 31, 33, 37,
    50, 74, 77, 86, 100
Morris, Robert, 34, 89
motives, 54, 62
mountains out of molehills, 23
Mount Vernon, viii, x, 62
Moustier, Comte de, 42, 51, 86, 95
Murray, William Vans, 38, 70
Muse, George, 27

national character, 100
national debt, 63. *See also* borrow-
    ing money; public credit
national interest, 50–51
national service, 63. *See also* duty;
    patriotism; public service
national university, 29
nature, 15, 63, 72, 75, 83, 99. *See also*
    environment; human nature
navy, 64
necessity, 9, 13, 30, 91, 101
negotiations, 64
Nelson, Thomas, 54
New Church in Baltimore, 82
Newenham, Edward, 54, 60, 81,
    97, 100
Newport, R.I., Hebrew Congrega-
    tion of, 82
New York: Council of Safety, 4;
    Provincial Congress, 90
newspapers, 75
North Carolina, governor and
    council of, 71

obedience, 64, 98; to government,
    43, 97; to military orders, 59
obstacles, 23
office holding, 71, 74, 75, 82
old age, 21, 85
opinions, 65–66; differences of, 25,
    39; international, 30–31; poli-
    tical, 71–72; religious, 81–82.
    See also advice, beliefs, public
    opinion, reputation
opponents, 66. *See also* enemies
optimism, 22, 66, 72
order, 14, 62

Paine, Thomas, vii
Papers of George Washington, xiv
parsimony, 34

[107]

Divine Providence; God; heaven; religious disputes; religious freedom

religious disputes, 81

religious freedom, 81–82

remedies, 82

remodeling, 82

representatives, 83

reproach, 83

republican form of government, 39, 53, 55, 83

reputation, 37, 50, 83–84. *See also* censure; defamation; popularity; slander

respect, 50, 84

rest, 92

retaliation, 84

retirement, 85

reverence, 40

Revolutionary War. *See* American Revolution; dissension; patriotism; soldier-citizen; soldiers and politicians; Valley Forge

revolutions, 85–86. *See also* American Revolution; discontent; turbulent times

reward, 27, 58, 67, 68

ridicule, 86

rights of conscience, 55

risk, 91

Rochambeau, Comte de, 31, 95

Rochefoucauld-Liancourt, Duc de la, 54

Rodgers, John, 67

Roman Catholics, 95

rudeness, 27

Rules of Civility and Decent Behavior in Company, xiii, 3, 8, 9, 11, 12, 15, 17, 18, 22, 23, 25, 27, 33, 35, 36, 40, 42, 48, 60, 67, 76, 83, 84, 86, 87, 91, 94

rum, 86, 98. *See also* drunkenness

rumors, 86. *See also* gossip; truth

Schuyler, Philip, 14, 22, 47, 69, 78, 101

science, 9, 87. *See also* mathematics

secrecy, 64, 87

self-deception, 21

self-interest, 87–88. *See also* interest; national interest

self-respect, 100

Senate, 67, 96

sermons, 88

sickness, 41, 48

silence, 22, 65, 88, 89

sincerity, 88–89

Sinclair, John, 4

sitting for portraits, 89

slander, 89. *See also* calumny; censure; defamation; lies

slavery, 89–90

society, 80

soldier-citizen, 80, 90

soldiers, 80, 90, 98. *See also* army; cowardice; danger; discipline; duty; mercenaries; military orders; officers; plundering; war

soldiers and politicians, 90

speech, 3, 22, 29, 40, 42, 87, 89, 98; and action, 91, 94; and thought, 91. *See also* argument; conversation; freedom of speech; language; propaganda; public speaking; silence; writing

spies, 91

spirit, 69

Spotswood, Alexander, 34, 66

Stewart, Robert, 70

Stirling, Lord, 32, 59

Stockton, Annis Boudinot, 6, 57, 71

Stone, John Hawkins, 7

strategy, 91–92

stress, 92

Strickland, William, 77

Stuart, David, 11, 62, 68, 96

success, 24, 83, 87, 92

Sullivan, John, 24, 30, 39

suspicion, 92, 102

system, 12, 93

talent, 50, 61

taxes, 93

teamwork, 93

tedium, 94

temptation, 57

thinking and acting, 94

thinking and speaking, 91, 94

Thurston, Charles Mynn, 53, 77, 96

time, 9, 43, 94–95

toleration, 95

traitors, 95

treason, 95

treaties, 95–96. *See also* foreign policy; international relations

Trumbull, John, 20

Trumbull, Jonathan, 29, 74, 92

Trustees of Washington Academy, 9

truth, 47, 86, 96

truths, 32, 99; mathematical, 57. *See also* maxims

turbulent times, 96

tyranny, 7